JIM BRANDENBURG

To the Top of the World

ADVENTURES WITH ARCTIC WOLVES

Edited by JOANN BREN GUERNSEY

WALKER AND COMPANY ✺ NEW YORK

First published in the United States of America in 1993 by Walker Publishing Company, Inc.;
first paperback edition published in 1995.

Published simultaneously in Canada by Thomas Allen & Son Canada, Limited, Markham, Ontario

Library of Congress Cataloging-in-Publication Data
Brandenburg, Jim.
   To the top of the world: adventures with Arctic wolves / Jim
Brandenburg: edited by JoAnn Bren Guernsey.
      p.   cm.
   Summary: A wildlife photographer records in text and photographs
a visit to Ellesmere Island, Northwest Territories, where he
filmed a pack of Arctic wolves over several months.
   ISBN 0-8027-8219-1. —ISBN 0-8027-8220-5 (lib. ed.)
   1. Wolves—Northwest Territories—Ellesmere Island—Juvenile
literature. [1. Wolves.] I. Guernsey, JoAnn Bren. II. Title.
QL737.C22B636   1993
599.74′442—dc20   93-12105
                                                                    CIP
                                                                    AC

ISBN 0-8027-7462-8 (paper)

Photograph on page 20 © Stephen Durst

~ Contents

Minus 60 degrees Fahrenheit; the orange glow is a product of the low-hanging March sun.

~ *Chapter 1*

THE ULTIMATE PHOTOGRAPH

The leader of the wolf pack glanced back at me as I scrambled after him across the ice. He didn't appear to sense any danger. He just looked curious, maybe even a little amused, as if saying to himself, "*That* odd creature is really trying to sneak up on *me*?"

It was crazy to think that anyone bundled up in Arctic gear could escape a wolf's notice. Wolves are one of the most perceptive animals on earth, with extraordinary senses. But I couldn't help myself. My heart pounded with excitement because I sensed something about this wolf, whom I had nicknamed Buster (after my father). He was about to present me with the chance to take the greatest photograph of my life.

Buster was leading the pack to a favorite spot, an iceberg on which they often spent their time exploring, howling with one another, goofing off, napping. Since it was April, the wolves' iceberg was still shackled to the land by an eight-foot crust of ice. The altitude is irresistible to Arctic wolves. They seem to *like* climbing to the tops of things. From the heights, they can survey the territory and keep an eye on new developments. They had littered the iceberg with droppings—a KEEP OUT sign to other packs. And to me.

Looking for tracks in full Arctic gear, which includes handmade Inuit mukluks.

1

Now I needed to find my perfect vantage point, too. As I crouched and lumbered across the dry, Arctic snow, it squeaked like Styrofoam under my feet. The wolves were some 150 yards away from me. So I settled against a six-foot pressure (ice) ridge and began to shoot photographs frantically. My powerful lenses made the wolves appear much closer than they were. As I reloaded my camera, Buster trotted over to a flat projection halfway up the iceberg. From this makeshift throne, he watched me. Suddenly, a single shaft of light illuminated the wolf while leaving the surrounding iceberg in blue, muted shadow. Nature had never provided me with a more perfectly composed photograph.

Buster sat there, in that perfect spot, for no more than thirty seconds. My thoughts raced ahead to when the editors at *National Geographic* would process my film. I was nervous and pessimistic about the outcome. Had the wind shaken the lens at the last second? Were the wolf's eyes open, or did I catch him blinking at the instant I snapped the shutter?

I found out later that, out of dozens of shots I'd taken of the lone wolf, only one turned out the way I had hoped it might.

Good photographs, like wolves, are elusive. Good photographs *of* wolves? Nearly impossible. I took this humbling realization as a challenge, which would inspire me in the long months to come.

Many people think Alaska is the most northerly part of North America, but Ellesmere Island, located in Canada's Northwest Territories, is actually several hundred miles farther north than any part of Alaska. From Ellesmere's tip to the North Pole measures some 500 miles across the Arctic Ocean.

During the winter, and for the first fifty or so days of "spring," such as it is, the water is frozen six to eight feet thick

Ice patterns shot from a plane over the Arctic Ocean.

Facing page: The perfect shot.

Fellow adventurer, Will Steger.

Facing page: The wolves have had no reason to fear humans on their remote island.

most of the way to the Pole. But this ice is nothing like the glassy ice familiar to skaters. Across its craggy, snow-blown surface, the ice cap is wrinkled with pressure ridges that make traveling on it difficult. Even worse are the frequent "leads"—yawning cracks in the ice that reveal open seawater.

I had taken other journeys into this treacherous, beautiful region during the first twenty years of my photographic career. Still, the *National Geographic* assignment to photograph the wildlife of Ellesmere Island, especially the wolves, was the fulfillment of a dream. And it all started when I first met my friend and fellow dreamer Will Steger. I think we each sensed something in the other: a kinship, a vision of the way we wanted to live our lives. Both of us had dreamed since childhood about testing ourselves, about danger, and about discovery. And we had found adventure wherever we could manage it.

The part of our conversation that I remember most vividly was about wolves. Arctic wolves. He had been dogsledding on Ellesmere with his wife two summers earlier. One morning they received a visitor.

"We woke up," Will told me, "and this large white head was staring at us through the flap of our tent. An Arctic wolf, as close to me as you are now. He showed no fear. He followed us for days, played with our dogs."

I was thrilled to think that a pack might exist that hadn't learned to fear humans. The images of that white wolf peering into Will Steger's tent and later playing with his dogs stuck stubbornly in my mind until I finally returned on assignment for *National Geographic* to follow the lives of these wolves for the whole Arctic summer. Even now, this time remains a highlight of my career, of my life.

The rocky outcropping at the den's entrance has been carved for eons by the winds of the High Arctic.

✍ Chapter 2
MEETING THE FAMILY

One of my first concerns was about how much I might interfere with the lives of these wolves. Would my presence cause them to abandon their den and disappear?

During most of the year, a wolf pack roams over its entire territory, making wolf study almost impossible. But each spring, the pack stays in or near one place. The mother must take to the den to have her pups, and the behavior of the whole pack revolves around feeding their young and ensuring their safety. This phenomenon makes study easier, but it also is a uniquely sensitive time.

How could I make it clear to the pack that I meant them no harm? That I would keep my distance and simply observe?

At first, I did not set up a permanent campsite in case the pack fled and moved to another den. I approached the den cautiously, alert to any signs that my presence might be causing stress in the pack. But the wolves never appeared overly nervous or bothered.

The den was set high on a hill. At its opening, rocks formed a kind of porch on which the pack members spent much of their time. The den opened into the earth from an entryway just large enough to fit snugly around the mother wolf. A hungry polar bear,

Adult wolf standing on the rooftop of the den.

The pups' narrow view of the world as seen from inside the den.

in other words, could not squeeze in to make a snack out of the growing pups. Inside, a clean, bug-free layer of sand covered the ground leading into a cave twenty feet deep. The rock walls provided excellent protection from the bitter cold.

Pups spend their first weeks inside the den huddled around their mother, and each other, for warmth. I was eager and impatient for my first look at them. When they finally appeared outside the den, they proved well worth the wait.

There were six puppies, cute little gray bundles of fur waddling after the adults on short, fuzzy legs and oversized paws. I guessed that they were about five weeks old. It seemed impossible that by winter they'd be running alongside their parents.

Several days later, I set up a camera about fifty yards from the den and was shooting photographs of the wriggling ball of pups. All seven adults looked in my direction, stretched, howled a few

The first lone excursion of one young pup.

The pups study the world outside their den.

times at the sky, and took off on a hunt. I couldn't believe it! Not one adult stayed behind to bark at me and keep me away from the den. They trusted me with their precious pups. Finally, after all those frustrating years of wolf pursuit, I would be able to get close to an entire pack. And what a family it was!

The way adult wolves are constantly caring for the young in their pack is only one of many similarities with human families. Wolves mate for life, and the whole pack functions as an extended family of aunts and uncles, brothers and sisters. They take turns baby-sitting and teaching the pups what they need to know.

Wolves have very individual personalities. Bison and musk-oxen all behave much the same within their herds. Not wolves. It probably has to do with their intelligence and gifts of perception.

At first, however, *my* perceptions were not up to the task of

The adult wolves are excellent caretakers of their young charges.

Scruffy is the lowest-ranking member of the adult hierarchy, but he basks in the respect and adoration of the pups.

Buster, the alpha male, sniffs a bouquet of Arctic poppies.

telling the seven wolves in this pack apart. But over the weeks of watching and listening to the wolves, I found myself more and more aware of their differences, like body scars, facial expressions, and coloring.

I also noticed that some of them behaved in dominant ways, bristling and cocky. Others were more submissive, cringing when in the presence of a "superior" and always trying to keep the peace. In other words, a hierarchy became apparent, a ranking of the wolves according to their power in relation to the others.

At the top was the alpha male, Buster. He was usually first to attack on a hunt and the first to eat after a kill. Buster's eyes were extremely expressive. Sometimes they were piercing, threatening. Other times they were amused, haughty, or quizzical. Weighing less than 100 pounds, he was not the largest of the pack. But he stood proudly on thin, long legs, taller than even the largest German shepherd.

Nearly his equal was the alpha female. I called her Midback because of a trail of dark fur running down her back. She was probably the most intelligent pack member. It was also clear that she was the *least* pleased to have me around. Midback's quickness and skill made her the best hunter among the pack.

Although scientists say that only the alpha pair has pups each spring, Midback was not the mother of the pups. There is no way to know why this alpha female did not give birth, but she was the most fiercely protective "parent" the pups had. She behaved like a dominant aunt who was often jealous of the pups' mother, whom I called, simply, Mom. Midback often rivaled Mom's authority over the pups.

Mom quickly became one of my favorites. She was a natural mother—gentle, tolerant, and devoted to the pups. Her facial expression can only be described as sweet and serene. And for some

Midback, the pack's best hare hunter, catches her prey and carries it with haughty pride to the grateful pups.

Mom's serene disposition makes her the most tolerant member of the pack.

Facing page: Scruffy tolerates nose-nibbling by the growing pups.

reason she seemed to have complete trust in humans. Maybe she simply got used to having me around because she was tied to the den.

The other wolf that could most often be found with the pups was my other favorite. He was an "adolescent" wolf, probably from the previous year's litter. His position in the pack was at the opposite end from the alpha pair—the bottom. I called him Scruffy because he was always a mess. His summer coat was scraggly, with huge balls of hair hanging from virtually every part of his hide.

There was a kind of goofiness about Scruffy that endeared him to me, especially since he tended to follow me around a lot. He was usually left behind from a hunt, but baby-sitting was the perfect job for him because of his playfulness. It also gave him the

At times, the usually playful Scruffy must show his dominance over the pups by exposing his teeth and growling.

chance to act dominantly over somebody, at least when Mom wasn't looking.

It was part of his job to play rough with the pups, knock them down hard enough to make them yelp. Though this kind of bullying may seem cruel, it is a necessary part of the pups' training. They have to learn the importance of knowing one's place in the hierarchy. This arrangement is crucial to the pack's unity and survival. Maintaining that ranking and its strict rules of behavior keeps the peace, avoids continual fights and injuries, maybe even death.

I knew less about the remaining three adults in the pack, mostly because they spent less time at the den site. Left Shoulder, a male named for a three-inch patch of missing fur on his left shoulder, was the largest, whitest wolf in the pack. Despite his size, he was submissive to the point of groveling in the presence of both Buster and Midback. The other two adults had even lower status in the pack, and I never got much of a sense of their personalities.

Many changes in the pack's membership would inevitably follow from one year to the next. But these seven adults and six pups made up the "family" as it existed one particular spring and summer on Ellesmere Island.

Facing page: Left Shoulder shows no sign of favoring the wounded shoulder for which he was named; the wound was probably caused by the horn or hoof of a musk-ox.

❧ Chapter 3

LIVING AS NEIGHBORS

While searching for an ideal campsite, I found a skull embedded in the powdery soil.

The story the skull told of the wolf's amazing survival skills intrigued me. Puncturing the lower jawbone was the tip of a musk-ox horn that had broken off, probably during combat. Bone tissue had grown thick across the point of injury, showing that he had lived for at least several months after the battle. The simple act of chewing must have been terribly painful, but his worn teeth indicated that he was very old when he died.

The discovery of this skull gave me an unusual glimpse into the harsh lives these wolves lead. It also provided a symbolic site on which to stake my own territorial claim for the spring and summer.

This setting was a deep valley about a quarter-mile east of the den. A pair of binoculars allowed me to keep track of the pack's activities. My presence did not seem to affect the wolves in a negative way. They made regular trips to the camp, apparently to satisfy their curiosity. My goal was to blend in, to lie low without trying to hide or trick the wolves. There was, however, one unavoidable exception to this approach. It was my means of transportation, the Suzuki all-terrain vehicle (ATV).

Facing page: Scruffy baby-sits puppies by the den's entrance.

Once a kill is made, the alpha pair eats first, followed by Mom (shown here), and then the others, in the pack's descending order of hierarchy.

A doomed calf is pulled down to its death.

swung her horns wildly, nearly hooking one of the wolves. It took only the split second in which the wolves loosened their grip on the calf for it to scramble alongside its mother back to the ring.

But the first calf was still hopelessly separated from the herd, and now the entire pack swarmed over it, biting away and eating its flesh for several minutes until, finally, the calf fell and died.

Very quickly, the alpha pair took control of the carcass, feasting while the rest of the pack fidgeted around the edges, whining for a share. After Buster and Midback finally showed signs of having had enough, the lower-ranking members came closer and closer, cringing and begging hungrily.

But Buster played out his role as leader a bit longer. He stood over the carcass, snapping his jaws at the others while they inched forward on their bellies and tilted their heads back. They each wore on their faces a nervous kind of grin. After a while, the other wolves drew close enough to lick the blood from Buster's muzzle.

At last, the alpha pair seemed to have had enough groveling from the others, and the carcass could be divided up. There would be nearly twenty pounds of meat for each wolf, and it took the pack two hours to reduce the calf to hide and bones.

After the feast, the wolves splashed in a nearby pond, drinking and washing off some of the blood from their fur. Then they wiped themselves by rolling around on the grass. Even after all this, however, each wolf wore a blood mask for several days.

The kill was about twenty miles from the den, so they did not rest long before heading back. After all, six hungry puppies were waiting for them. I raced ahead with my equipment so I could record the next part of the feeding as well. The feast would be regurgitated for two reasons: to share the meat with the puppies and to store extra, undigested meat for future use.

At the den, the pups heard the older generation howling from

Throughout their engorgement, the wolves make trips to a nearby stream to drink the water that is necessary for digesting so much meat; they also wash the blood from their coats before it has a chance to dry and harden.

I hesitate to dwell on this episode because wolves already have a bad enough reputation without any stories of imperiled photographers. The widely held opinion of wolves is that they are extremely dangerous. For centuries, children have been told fairy tales with wolves as the villains. Thanks in part to movies and books, the mere sound of a wolf howling in the distance is often enough to inspire terror. The wolf, in many cultures, is a symbol of evil.

This exaggerated fear of attack has caused so many wolves to be trapped, shot, or poisoned that, on many continents, they have been almost wiped out. In the United States, wolves today occupy less than 1 percent of their former territory.

The fact is that all the countless wolf–human interactions have resulted in virtually no recorded accounts of unprovoked attacks by healthy wolves. Our chances of being attacked by a fellow human are vastly greater than any risk posed by a wolf. Every major predator in North America, from mountain lions to grizzly bears, will occasionally strike out against humans without provocation, but wolves will not. I have asked a number of biologists about this, but there appears to be no logical explanation.

Facing page: The ever-confident Buster appears to take great pleasure in finding unusual situations.

As the summer draws to a close, the fur of the half-grown pups starts to whiten, beginning with their faces; once they reach full maturity, their coats will remain white all year long.

ᔍ Chapter 7

GOOD-BYE

Breaking camp at the end of a two-month stay is never easy. A small mountain of equipment had to be packed up and transported from the campsite to a landing strip six miles away. From there I'd arranged for a Twin Otter (a small plane with skis for wheels) to pick me up and fly me home, and I anticipated this with a mixture of excitement and regret.

It was now the end of August, and the first prewinter snows were beginning to fall. The puppies had grown a lot, and their fur, which had been grayish at birth, had given way to a buff orange that provided perfect camouflage against the fall vegetation. The whitening of their fur was already becoming visible, especially around their faces.

But the pups were still less than half the size of the adults and were unable to catch their own prey. They had so much left to learn before they could survive on their own. In the high Arctic the seasons don't give puppies much time to stay puppies. By autumn, I had already watched the adults urging the puppies on short expeditions, but the greatest distance they had traveled was about half a mile.

As the pack watched my preparations to leave, I took several photographs. I knew these final images would take on special im-

For two weeks, the wolves abandoned their den, apparently to allow parasites and other pests to die in the absence of warm-blooded hosts; the substitute den is a rock pile with cavities just large enough for the puppies to wriggle inside for shelter.

portance because I would never see these wolves all together again. Almost certainly, I knew, the pups would remain with the pack until the following spring. At that time, when the mating season began again, most of the puppies who survived the winter would be banished from the pack to make room for the new arrivals. Perhaps some of these survivors would form successful packs of their own in nearby territories. More likely, though, given the harshness of the habitat, they would perish.

So I felt tremendous sadness the morning I left with my last load of supplies. I looked over at the pack and said good-bye.

But a few hours later, just before I was about to climb aboard the plane, I noticed some movement at the distant end of the runway. I couldn't believe my eyes: It was the wolves, and not just the adults. They had brought the puppies the entire six miles with them. As the adults sat watching the plane, the pups tugged at one another and played wolf tag.

The sight of them left me speechless. Was it coincidence that they had picked this day to take the pups on their first long-distance walk? The other explanation, that they had actually come to say good-bye, seemed impossible. All I know is that I found this gesture, whatever the reasons for it, deeply moving.

The Arctic wolves changed my life. Their story was the highlight of my career as a wildlife photographer. They gave me the chance to achieve a dream. I hope that by sharing their lives with the world, and disproving some of the myths about wolves, I can begin to pay them back.